Hollywood Stars

Jean Mulatier

Text research by
Jean Mulatier, Georg F W Tempel

RAVETTE BOOKS

THE STARS IN CLOSE UP

CARICATURE: Disfigured surgery involving the making of incisions with a sword disguised as a scalpel; every effort must be made to avoid departing too far from the original, as this could contribute to a deterioration in the likeness — and interest.

In each of the caricatures contained in this book, I have tried to capture the best possible likeness of the person in question by exaggerating certain important physical characteristics. I have not set out to make these individuals unappealing in any way by emphasising only their so-called 'faults'. Nobody is that imperfect!

The caricature is the opposite of a *distorting* mirror in that it has to start from the basis of what the model is truly like. That is the key to a good likeness. It is rather an *enlarging* mirror which simply highlights certain aspects of the person's face. It does this by altering the proportions of the various parts of the face according to how important they are in providing a decent likeness.

It is the art of blowing up and reducing at the same time — blowing up what seems to be fundamental and reducing what seems to be less so. Just imagine having to put together the pieces of a jigsaw puzzle, some of whose pieces have been enlarged and others made smaller! That might give you an idea of the sort of headache it is! The funny thing is that, in many cases, a caricature can easily pass for a straight portrait; it is also one of those times when the imitation can actually be more *convincing* than the original. Another way of looking at caricatures is as forgeries which simultaneously pastiche the original model — it is certainly the only kind of forgery that deliberately brings differences into relief. The caricature is an unusual art form and never fails to raise a smile.

It is preferable not to exaggerate the exaggeration too much; otherwise, there is a danger of descending into cruelty and, in so doing, failing to capture the likeness. The real problem is knowing the extent to which it is possible to go too far. The slightest deviation of the pen can nudge the drawing towards a particular shade of expression, or even towards non-likeness. This is caricaturing at its most tentative, and is based on the one golden rule that applies to drawing and everything else: THE MOST IMPORTANT THING IS TO WORK OUT WHAT IS MOST IMPORTANT — AND TO GIVE IT PRIDE OF PLACE. The two or three things you first notice about someone are bound to be the first few things you see in the finished caricature. The caricature will also be stuffed with imperfections in spite of all the perfectionism — perhaps because of it, who knows?

These days, the word 'caricaturing' has come to mean 'at odds with the truth'. What that comes down to is a caricaturish view of caricatures, and that in turn can end up being more like the truth, even though it has been achieved through exaggeration.

When we like something, we exaggerate. I exaggerate what I like in peoples faces by putting them under the microscope. All these drawings have been conceived and executed as *works of homage* to the masterpieces of nature — which is what these faces are. This is particularly true of the faces of certain actors. The impact that some of these faces have on the general public is not always a consequence of their fame; it is often the cause. A caricature is only offensive when it is not a good likeness, and it goes without saying that it will always be less of a good likeness than the original. They say that nothing resembles a subject better than a caricature . . .! Well, after the subject itself, let's say!

The combined influence of American cinema actors (''The Magnificent Seven'' and a few others — there are also a few faces like that of Steve McQueen that I don't go overboard over) and the drawings of the great Mort Drucker in *Mad* made me want to do these caricatures. Actors had already confirmed my early yearnings to go in for drawing — although I am not quite sure about Peter Pan being an actor, which is what I thought at the time. There is something impertinent about looking at someone's face in close up as if it were a great expanse of countryside. On the other hand, is it fair to criticise a spectator for having a pair of eyes?

The fact that stars are attractive makes us want to get close to them, and of course we have also become familiar with them through the huge size of the cinema screen. The cinema teaches us to go for faces because the appeal of an actor's face is one of the ways she/he becomes interesting, even if the actor in question is playing a negative character. Many actors including Bogart and Depardieu have made their names with the film-going public on the basis of tough guy roles. The former, in particular, was 'the one we love to hate' for a long time until he became the one we just loved. Some faces are real gifts of nature — for the caricaturist, at least. In those cases, nature has already done half the work for us.

As far as really good-looking stars are concerned, the pen does not flow nearly so easily when the features are nice and smooth. It is a well-established fact that the delicate faces of women and children lend themselves even less. 'Caricaturing' beauty by making it even more beautiful is an ambition that must have sent more than one person to a psychiatric hospital. As perfection is not to be found in this world, it is much more relaxing to resign oneself to not being its representative on earth. That is one reason why there are so few women in this album. Another reason is to spare them the shock treatment which is anyway much more appropriate to the tough guys of the so-called 'stronger' sex. I am not sure what some people will make of that. At all events, this minority of female stars is in line with the ratio of one woman to every seven men in the real world!

Another great discovery that I have made while producing this book is that the well-known faces of the cinema can be divided into two categories according to their eyebrows. The two groups may be called the beseechers and the frowners. The circumflex accent (i.e. A-shaped) eyebrows of the former describe the curve of a question mark on the owners' foreheads. This is the source of the slightly begging look we see on the faces of John Wayne, Roger Moore, Clark Gable and particularly Humphrey Bogart — not to mention the positively miserable expressions of James Dean and Woody Allen. (Let us not forget that Bogart would not allow photos of his 'lived-in face' to be touched up. Caricaturists will be eternally grateful to him for that.) This expression of vulnerability moves women to pity and makes them want to mother these stars. The actors always seem to be posing questions. Jimmy Dean seems to be asking himself, 'Where am I? Where do I come from? Where am I going?', and Woody Allen is replying 'The answer is Yes, but what was the question?', although he can't stop himself asking another question in turn. As the questioner-in-chief, Allen is to the beseechers what Alain Delon is to the French frowners. He surely would have given anything to be a giver of replies — a frowner, in other words — like Clint Eastwood, Schwarzi, Michael Douglas, Kevin Costner and Tom Cruise.

Between their severe, V-shaped eyebrows, the frowners have small vertical lines that look like exclamation marks. For some reason, frowners are also go-getters. They are the *imposers*, while beseechers are the *proposers*; the former are pro-active and interventionist, while the latter are passive and contemplative. To put it in another way, we have winners and losers — the only exception being John Wayne, a rare example of a beseecher who is also a winner. Another actor worth taking a look at is Charles Bronson, an unusual case of the beseeching frowner; he frowns with his eyebrows and beseeches with his 'thatched roof' eyelids.

Between these two categories, we have the Brandos, de Niros and all the unclassifiable individuals whose wide range of expression enables them to travel between one group and the other. They have suppleness and subtlety. Apparent frowners like Sean Connery, Jack Nicholson and Dustin Hoffman have too much of a sense of humour to stay serious for long. Basically, though, the two main groups are also comedians — and the collection in this book includes all types. The sureness of the frowners puts them in the same category as Pierrot-type clowns, while the uneasiness of the beseechers aligns them with other kinds of clown that are more likely to get a kick in the backside. Cosmetics manufacturers have decreed that female beauty is incompatible with wrinkles, and this means that screen goddesses have to have inexpressive foreheads. It also keeps the doors of the eyebrow clubs firmly closed to them. Now that's a real shame!

The last discovery I made while doing this book is that the majority of the great stars became stars with the help of an often surprisingly rich cocktail of talents. The ideas attributed in this book to the likes of Brando, Marilyn, Marlene, Depardieu and Hoffman attest to impressive verbal skills; these include common sense, humour and poetic intuitions — and threads of premonition as in the case of James Dean. So I had all these pearls at my disposal, and the challenge consisted of putting some or all of the necklace back together again. The puzzle of the physical portaits on the right-hand pages is answered in the puzzle of the personal portaits on the left-hand pages. This is something like a verbal self-caricature: it is also couched in just enough self-mockery for the actor in question to swallow the bitter pill of home truths — and make it palatable to others. The spirit is on the left, the body is on the right. As Woody Allen asks, 'If the body and the spirit are separate, which is preferable?'

One thing is for sure. Some people *radiate* in the real sense of the word, and irresistibly attract looks. Marilyn's masseur (lucky man!) claimed that she even radiated in the dark! People who light up inside have a huge advantage over their poor colleagues who only light up internally with the help of external spotlights. That must be the reason why stars are defined as 'celestial bodies emitting their own light'.

Jean Mulatier

ACKNOWLEDGEMENTS

'Any writer, musician, painter or actor will tell you, when they take a look at their work after it's finished, they know it could have been done better. But, when all is said and done, all you can do is to say to yourself, "Well, I did my job. It's all over and done with. Either they'll like it or they won't." '
James Dean

'Tell me who you dedicate your books to, and I'll tell you who you are.' *Simon Edgar Funkel*

As they say at the Oscar ceremony, I'd like to thank the whole team who helped me and supported me (sometimes without realising it) in the production of this film — sorry, book!

These remarks are directed to beauty in general, and in particular to the internal and external beauty of all the caricatures on the pages coming up. So, thanks to Catherine, Colline and to:

Omar Ali-Shah, Peter Allen, Animalia, France, Bruno & Luis Ansa, Jacques & Jeanne Arbez, Sylvain Augier, Hartmut Becker, Elmer Bernstein, Georges Bertrand, Laurence Billard, Huguette, Sandrine & Eloi Bimont, Bobette, Richard Bohringer, Dr Jean-Paul Bonnefont, Agnès Borie, Jean-Louis Bory, François Boucq, Jean-Marc Bretnacher, Marlon Brando, Claire Bretecher, Charles Bronson, Dik Browne, Anke, Calvin, Canard & Pimpon, Caroline, Marguerite Carvallo, John Cassavetes, Carlos Castaneda, Claude & Irina Chauchet, Alain Cicerone, James Coburn, Paul Coker Jr, Liliane Couturier, Françoise, Joséphine, Abdel & Frédéric Dard, Patrick Deblaere, Pascal De Duve, Thierry Defert, Louis De Funès, Nicole De La Margé, Jean-François Deniau, Élaine Depondt, François De Roubaix, Paul Derouet, Diogène, Jean-Pierre Dirick, Walt Disney, Dominique, Joy & Gilles, Kirk Douglas, Mort Drucker, Véronique & Pierre Dumoulin, Jacques Dutronc, Robert Duvall, Editons Sévigny, Elisete, Philippe Enjolras, Tatiana, Natacha & Sacha Faria, Pierre Ferrand, Jean-Marie Fitère, Liliane & André Franquin, Frazette, Lena Frias, Roger Gaillard, Anne-France Gallois, Thierry Geoffrois, Georg Gerster, Gilberte, Anne & René Goscinny, Gotlib, Lawrence Grobel, Emmanuel Guibert, Alain Guichard, Gutemberg, Gerhard Haderer, Johnny Hart, Audrey Hepburn, Hergé, Margarethe Hubauer, Les Humains Associés, Ben Hur, John Hurt, Gérard Jalbert, Jean-Claude, Marlène Jobert, Katie Joffo, Don Juan (Matus), Marcel Jullian, Hank Ketcham, Krishnamurti, Sebastian Krüger, Monique Lalaison-Nguyen, Burt Lancaster, Lino Landolfi, Suzy Lapetite, Janine & René Leguet-Thiéry, Sergio Leone, Levine, Jordi Longaron, Bernadette Von Lonski, Mimi Lopin, Mohamed Lounef, Lucques, Dino Lupatelli, Ali McGraw, Terl McLuhan, Jeff McNelly, Melly, Neile, Teri, Chad & Steve McQueen, The Magificent Seven, Mamie, Mandryka, Claude Marin, Marol, Richard Martens, Jacques Martin, Lee Marvin, Le Masque et La Plume, Walter Matthau, Barbara Minty, Moebius, Dr Monin, Patrice Mouilleseaux, Mordillo, Ennio Morricone, Pr Munich, Mucha, Nicolaz, Nicephore Niepce, Jennifer O'Neill, Brant Parker, Sam Peckinpah, Peyo, Bill Plymton, Michel Polnareff, Prechtl, Première, Proccopio, Jacques Rampal, Charlotte Rampling, Josh Randell, Danielle Rapoport, Redon, Ricord, Chantal Ros, Marie-Noëlle Rousselot, Saadi, Robert Sabatier, Pr Saudubray, Charles Schulz, George C Scott, Ronald Searle, Chief Seattle, Sénèque, Jeanne-Marie Sens, Serguei (& Françoise), Erich Sokol, Sorel, Spirou, John Sturges, Studio, Summer of 42, Georg Tempel, Thâ, Tillieux, Tintin, Laurence Trell, Annie Trimouillat, Lao Tseu, Tchouang Tseu, Uderzo, Ulysse, Peter Ustinov, Brigitte Verdeaux, Gisella Vetter, Eli Wallach, Wasterlein, Bill Watterson, Christian Wendel, Isabelle Willemetz, Patrick Witzig, Claude Wolf, Stevie Wonder, Yrrah, Yveline, Chantal Zerbib, Ziraldo, Zorglub . . .

and all their mums and dads without whom none of them would be on the list in the first place . . . and also to all those who are not on the list at all, either because I forgot or there was not enough room.

CONTENTS

'My parents lived together for forty years — and they did so out of pure animosity.'

'All my best ideas come from mental tortures you wouldn't credit!'

'Another year of psychoanalysis — and I'm off to Lourdes.'

' "Hannah and her Sisters" is more optimistic than I would have liked. Where did I go wrong? The most optimistic moments are the ones I think I messed up.'

'Life is hard and Darwinian. The wolves are gobbling one another up. He who strikes, wins. Nobody could care a damn about lofty aspirations. You have nothing to guide you except your own morality. And if you lose that compass, your existence becomes terrifying. Anyone at all now may be hunted down as the guilty party. Take the Jews, for instance. Imagine a planet without them! Even if there was just one nationality, we would think up new reasons for exterminating our neighbours, left-handers, sopranos, lovers of pink cars and so on.'

'I loathe reality, even though I realise it's the only place where I can get a decent steak.'

'Never has pornography laid out its stall so shamelessly! And to make matters worse, the films are all fuzzy!'

'My sole regret in life is not having been someone else — either that or Ursula Andress' tights.'

'What wouldn't I give to be a genius like Marlon Brando! But would *he* want to be in *my* shoes? He'd have to be mad . . . or want to be thin!'

'I wanted to be a spy, but you had to swallow microfilm and my doctor wouldn't allow it.'

'I've always had a weakness for kamikaze women. They crash their planes and self-destruct, but they also crash their planes on top of you!'

'Even when I was still quite little, I was always attracted by the wrong one. When my mother took me to see "Snow White", I immediately fell for the wicked queen.'

'I can't claim to be the greatest lover in the world, but coming in seventh isn't too bad.'

'It's better to have money than to be poor, if only for financial reasons.'

'Eternity takes a long time, particularly towards the end.'

WOODY ALLEN

'He was the kind of individualist that today's young people would like to be, but which they'll never be able to become as long as they dream up nonsense like the Bogart cult.' *Lauren Bacall*

'His great fundamental quality was his ruggedness. Even when he was dressed up, I felt I could have struck a match on his cheek.' *Sir Peter Ustinov*

'Nothing can happen to your mug to make it any worse!' they shouted to him in the production company.

When the producer Jack Warner asked, 'Who'd want to kiss a face like his?', they say that Ingrid Bergman replied, 'Me!'.

'In my first thirty-four films, I was knocked to the ground twelve times, electrocuted or hanged twelve times, and I escaped from prison nine times. I played more scenes writhing in agony on the ground than I did on my feet. My main difficulties were working out new ways of saying ''Aaaargh!'' and coughing up blood. I have invented several new ways of clutching my stomach, and I use some of them to this day.'

'I'm not a tough guy. I just pretend to be. I am quite well mannered. It's all to do with my upbringing. But in today's rat race, it can be difficult not to lose your manners.'

'There's only one way of surviving getting an Oscar, and that's not to try and get another one. Otherwise, you spend the rest of your life turning down scripts while you look for the great role that will give you that second Oscar.'

'The only honest way to tell who is the best actor is to get them all to do Hamlet.'

'If you want to succeed, try and become an actor, not a star.'

'I really have to be able to act to drink the coloured water they give you and pretend it's real whisky!'

'Class is something money can't buy. You don't acquire it like a suntan. I know! I was born with it!'

'When you believe in something, fight for it — even if there's a chance you'll come off worse as a result. It'll be worth it in the long run. And don't forget to put a bit of money to one side for a rainy day.'

HUMPHREY BOGART

'You're not at all an unpleasant American after all!' remarked a journalist. 'And when did you last see me without any clothes on?' Brando replied.

'Hollywood is a cultural cemetery. The cinema is an industry, not art.'

'No film is a work of art.'

'There are no artists these days. Just people like you and me who make dough.'

'I do not have the moral strength to refuse piles of money.'

'Cinema actors are not artists; they're psychopaths. If you ask them what they like, their replies are simply staggering. Acting is a bottom-of-the-pile job which gives people a chance to perfect their self-satisfaction. I no longer have anything else to prove.'

'Everybody's an actor. We spend all day acting.'

'The greatest actor is my dog. He pretends to love me when he's hungry.'

'I'd like to be a bull. First, I'd grab the picador. Then, I'd run after the matador until he shat in his pants, then I'd impale his arsehole on one of my horns and parade round the ring.'

'I'd have liked to have been a caveman. To find the denominator that was common to all men before we started talking rubbish . . . Men are afraid of women because they elevate them and depend on them . . . And mothers treat their children in the way men treat women. (He/She's *my* baby!)'

'No people has oppressed another people as much as the American people have oppressed the Indians. Almost 400 treaties have been signed, but *not one* has been observed! There are fourteen million Indians to the north and south, and yet they are the only one of the five great races of the world that is not represented at the UN. For the last 200 years, we have been silently exterminating a people from the face of the earth, and nobody gives a damn! It's obscene! We must never give up the struggle. Each time we suffer a set back, we learn that little bit more. The only way to solve problems is to tackle them head on. We need to find solutions, even if they seem unworkable. It's better than sitting around doing nothing.'

'What rich people do is to edge further and further away from parts of the world that are dangerous . . . until they eventually reach a desert island.'

MARLON BRANDO

'There are only seven stars left in the world, and Sean Connery is one of them.' *Steven Spielberg*

'At first, I was worried he was too young to play my father as he was only twelve years older than me. But acting with him was really like building something together. When one of us needed something, the other provided it. Sean knows how to knock the ball back to you, and he also indicates the direction he's hitting it.'
Harrison Ford

'Perhaps I'm not a good actor, but I would be even worse at doing anything else.'

'There's one major difference between James Bond and me! *He* is able to sort out problems!'

'People used to call me Bond in the street. It was impossible to avoid crowds of people all over the place and blinding flashguns. The Beatles had to run the gauntlet as well, but at least there were four of them!'

'As far as I'm concerned, Bond is over and done with. You need a younger actor now, about thirty-five — Mel Gibson perhaps . . .'

'I was in "Zardoz". I took over from Burt Reynolds who, I think, took ill after reading the script.'

'I met my wife through playing golf. She is French and couldn't speak English and I couldn't speak French, so there was little chance of us getting involved in any boring conversations — that's why we got married really quickly.'

'You know, the Oscar I was awarded for "The Untouchables" is a wonderful thing, but I haven't changed and I can honestly say that I'd rather have won the US Open Golf Tournament.'

'I originally thought of giving the Oscar statuette to my wife, but then I found out I could get more than $15,000 for it!'

'I am not an Englishman, I was never an Englishman, and I don't ever want to be one. I am a Scotsman! I was a Scotsman and I will always be one.'

SEAN CONNERY

'To play Elliott Ness, we needed an actor who had the substance, charm and simplicity of Steve McQueen.'
Producers of 'The Untouchables'

'Steve is my favourite actor. He has had a big influence on me. When I made "Bodyguard", it was like paying homage to my childhood hero.'
Kevin Costner

'I'd loved to be hired to do nothing but Westerns for five years. Unfortunately, I was born thirty years too late.'

'It was through making good films that I underwent my apprenticeship in moral values. Honour and loyalty touch me and attract me in the same way a pretty woman attracts looks. That is true even when I am trying to entertain rather than give lessons.'

' "Dances with Wolves" is my love letter to the past and to my Cherokee grandfather.'

'My only policy is respect for other people. Our planet's future is our children's future, and I am anxious to leave them somewhere decent to live.'

'Being a celebrity puts you at the mercy of people who can walk all over you. But the price you pay is high. Getting out of the house is quite a feat! I am harassed by autograph hunters, and journalists ask for my opinion on everything! Actors are accorded too much attention and too much importance. In practice, I am paid $100,000 for my work and $900,000 for not having a private life any more. I struggle to live a normal life in abnormal circumstances. Perhaps being famous means you've been a little too lucky. It is by no means certain that I will continue doing this kind of work forever.'

'My greatest quality as an actor? Standing up to the producer! In "Robin Hood", I refused to put on the green tights that Errol Flynn had worn. And if I can choose in a story between putting my arms round a woman and knocking someone off a horse, I'll choose the horse!'

KEVIN COSTNER

'He's a workaholic. He gets up at half past four in the morning, and never even stops for lunch!'
Dustin Hoffman

'He is quite remarkable — an extremely courageous actor, who knows no fear. I think that he will outlive his youth, which is not the case with many actors of his generation. *Paul Newman*

'I very nearly became a priest. I had to choose between the cloth . . . and adventure. But there was never any real doubt in my mind — adventure won!'

'My first real friends date from my time in the seminary. We had a really wild time together!'

'When school was over, I used to run home as fast as my legs could carry me because my sister's girl friends practised on me at kissing boys!'

'I remember the first time I met my agent. I was wearing a velvet jacket I'd had for two years and I said to him, ''I don't care whether I earn a lot of money or not. What matters more than anything else is being proud of what I have accomplished during the day.'' '

'My mother was very excited. She said to me, ''It's your agent on the phone!'' He had called to say I had got my first important role. I jumped up with such enthusiasm that I banged my head. I almost knocked myself out and collapsed to the ground. The whole family danced with joy.'

'When I started filming ''Cocktail'', Paul Newman sent me a six-pack and said, ''You're always working. I want you to sit down and take the weekend off. I want you to have all these beers.'' I did calm down — just a bit.'

'It's better to do something you believe in and like, because if it turns out to be a disaster, you haven't lost everything.'

'Even if I were to lose everything tomorrow, they'll never be able to take away from me what I have learned.'

'When I'm 70, I want to be able to turn round and tell myself that I didn't waste a single one of my opportunities.'

TOM CRUISE

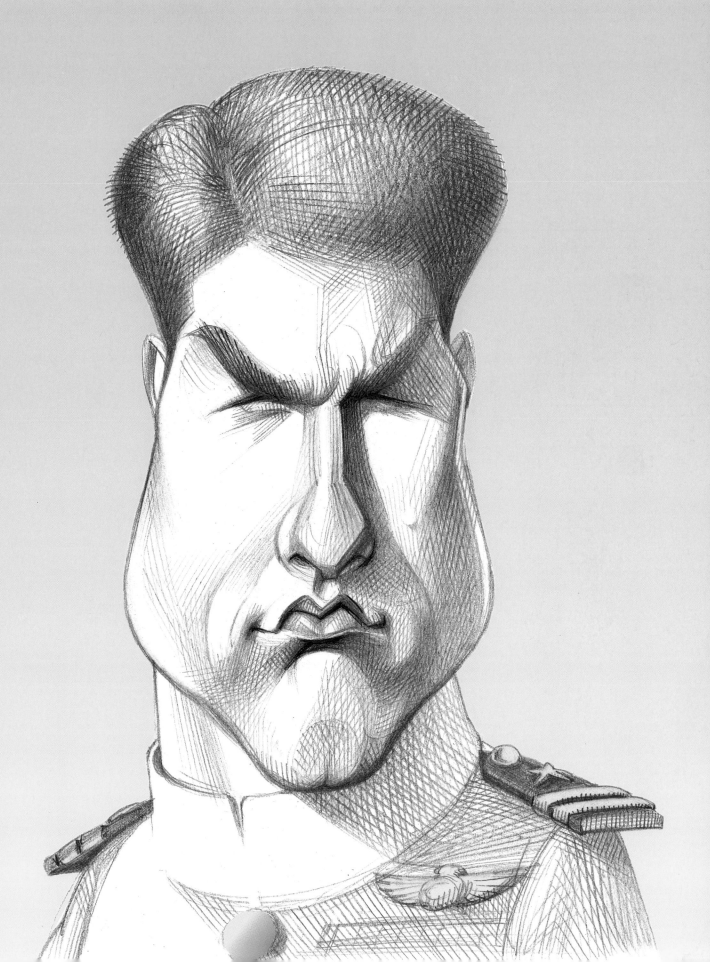

'Something that's very comforting about stars that have vanished from the scene early on is that there's no chance of them disappointing us.'   *Kay Kendall*

'I think my life story is so sinister that I can't talk about it without some serious background music — the Funeral March, perhaps!'

'When my mother died, I was still very young, and I spent hours crying on her grave. "Ma!" I used to weep. "Why did you leave me? I need you!" Now, though, it's "You'll see! I'll show you!" '

'I'm going to be the greatest!'

'I'm going to be as famous as Brando . . . a superstar, a Hollywood great.'

'I don't just want to be the best. I want to be so great that the rest of them are in a totally different league.'

'I'm too young and too stupid.'

'I don't want to ruin my health — I've done three films inside two years.'

I'm washed out.'

'I started work on "Giant" immediately after I'd finished "Rebel Without a Cause", a long and difficult film. I should simply have walked out — I'm quite sure of that!'

'There is no such thing as greatness in this world.'

'The only greatness is immortality.'

'You know, the producer's terrified I'm going to kill myself! Isn't that incredible? You've seen that article in Photoplay with a photo of me in a racing car, and a caption saying, "Film studios fear young tearaway will kill himself in road accident!" '

'I used to put my foot down hard. I used to take stupid risks on the road. Now I'm, very, very careful. Remember, drive slowly! The life you save may be *mine*!'
(*TV clip on road safety put out 13 days before his accident. The original text had "may be <u>yours</u>".*)

JAMES DEAN

'This job toughens women and feminises men . . . Women these days are warriors. And Catherine is one of them. Not armed to the teeth. On the contrary — very sensitive and human. But, unusually, she is also brave enough to expose herself. She goes into battle facing enemy fire, and does not make compromises with the century we live in.'

'Gainsbourg said you walked like a soldier, Mastroiani said you were stiff and ungainly. I've never seen you complain during filming . . . You are the man I would like to be. I want these qualities of yours which are given to men, and are yet so rarely found in them — more responsible, more powerful, better protected than actors. Less vulnerable. This paradox must surely be true femininity.'

Gérard Depardieu

'Like many actors, Gérard is a very feminine man . . . All directors who work with him are in love with him. The two of us work well together — it's the chemistry between us . . . We must have had a marvellous time together in a former life . . .!'

'I've always thought of physical beauty as something of a threat . . . After all, the devil dresses up in the most extraordinary disguises! If you're good-looking on the outside, you ought to be better-looking on the inside, except that that's even more unfair — almost intolerable!'

'I like it when people say I'm beautiful, but at the same time I've never really believed it. Not because I'm modest, but because I think rationally. Perhaps I look at myself more critically . . . You've got to be a certain age to find a philosophy that deals with that sort of thing . . . Looks are not so easy to live with, whatever they are. You've got to try and forget all about them.'

'When I see a photo of someone, it's both him and not him. The picture takes us back to something we have had a presentiment of, but never properly grasped. It's a bit like looking through a magnifying glass: you see things that are really there, but they are out of shape; sometimes they are more beautiful, sometimes less so . . .'

'If there had been no such thing as the cinema, I could have slept through my whole life like Sleeping Beauty. I need to be moving about to be sure that I'm still alive. Otherwise, I'm like those clocks whose pendulums slowly stop swinging. I'm not going to wait for the fire to go out before I go looking for wood.'

'The little girl I once was is still there . . . What I like about life now is what attracted me when I was ten or twelve. If I am attracted to something, nothing is going to stop me. It's like a magnet. I cannot resist the irresistible.'

'I sometimes get very frightened — terrified, in fact. I am shy when I have to meet other people. I often blush. I would prefer to go pale. It's more discreet.'

On hearing that French people had voted her their favourite star in a 1993 survey, Catherine Deneuve smiled and said, 'I represent for them a kind of immutable reality, if only because I have been imposing myself on them in my films for so many years, and they're now finding it difficult to find anyone else!'

CATHERINE DENEUVE

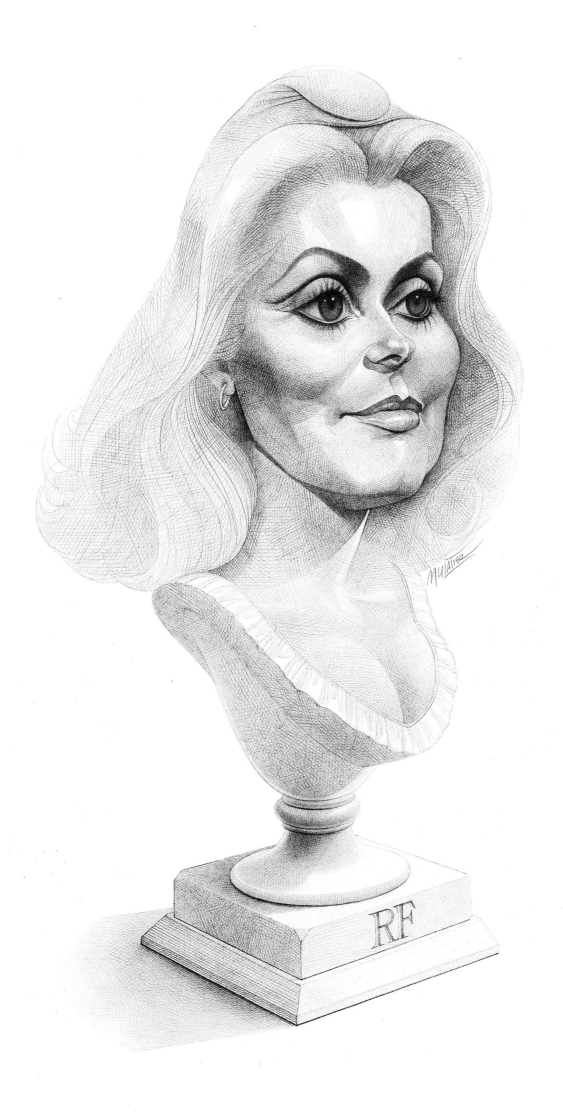

'The greatest living actor is de Niro, which fortunately, he doesn't realise.' *Marlon Brando*

'He always turned his back on the camera, as he realised that the less he is seen on screen, the more powerful his presence becomes. I used to say to him, ''No, Bob! turn round just a little . . . we can't just see your back through the whole film!'' ' *Sergio Leone*

'He is a real perfectionist. He trained himself up to box like a pro for ''Raging Bull''. Then, to show how far the old champion had declined, he put on 25 kilos! For the role of Al Capone in ''The Untouchables'', he even ordered the same silk pants from the gangster's official supplier, and had his head shaved for hours. ''One single hair too many and it all looks artificial,'' was his excuse, and then went off to have his nostrils enlarged for three hours every day! But more than anything else, he lost 15 kilos — and was sorry that he hadn't managed more. 'Putting on weight is depressing,' he admitted in the end. 'I'll never do it again.'

'When Martin Scorsese asked me to do ''The Last Temptation of Christ'', I didn't know what to say, because it wasn't my kind of film. At the time, my head was shaved. I took off my hat and said, ''Do I look like Jesus!'' But if he'd insisted — as a friend — I'd have made the film . . . I throw myself totally into every film I do.'

'He would go into training for weeks on end in order to multiply loaves,' sighed a critic.

'He is so human, he would have been simply divine!' *Film critic*

'I've always wanted to be a director — so as to be able to get other parts of my brain working.'

'An actor is someone who . . . er . . . looks for . . . um . . . Well, words aren't that important, are they?'

'In behaviour you can do a lot without saying anything. More with one eyebrow than in ten lines of dialogue.'

'The cinema is an illusion, but it isn't for me. If you do something over and over again, it might get better.'

'The important thing is to surprise the director. Most of them content themselves with the minimum.'

ROBERT DE NIRO

'He has the violence of a colossus and the fragility of a child . . . Depardieu knows his own soul, but it does not go with his looks. He sometimes gives the impression of stifling people. When he isn't working, he is like a caged lion.'

Jean-Paul Rappeneau, Director of "Cyrano de Bergerac"

'I must take after Cyrano in some way . . . All actors are like that. The business of acting, the way we expose ourselves — that's Cyrano all over. In fact, the whole character is a layabout who wants to say "I love you". What they do not know about is the drama of layabouts. There's a bit of Cyrano in all of us.'

'I have more than physical complexes. I can't stand myself! Fortunately, there are some people who help me . . . When I removed the false nose I wore for Cyrano — *that* was when I felt *really* disfigured!'

'That's got to be the reason why I became an actor. To be different from what I seemed to be. I was automatically taken for a layabout.'

'It's a good job I got into acting — otherwise I would probably have ended up as a killer.'

'I don't understand women. Just look at me — does a sex symbol really look like this?'

'Projects are like boilers. You have to feed them and go looking for wood to keep them going . . . I finished "Green Card" on 18 June, and on 22 June I was on the set of "Uranus". I was exhausted. People were saying, "What's the matter with Depardieu! Is he in a bad mood about something?" Depardieu was just dead on his feet!'

'Actors are both discreet and courageous. They spend all their time repeating things. It's exhausting repeating things over and over again. In psychiatric hospitals, they give you sedatives to stop you repeating things!'

'In a world that is increasingly bereft of femininity, I insist on keeping my dressmaker's and poet's soul.'

GÉRARD DEPARDIEU

'Marlene Dietrich . . . Your name begins with a caress and ends with the crack of a whip . . . Your voice and the way you look are of the Lorelei; but the Lorelei was dangerous, and you are not, because the secret of your beauty lies in your heart.'
Jean Cocteau

'My conception of Marlene was my own. She had nothing to do with it whatsoever. She did not even know herself what she was doing. To other people, she was a myth, but she wasn't to me. The real myth was me behind the camera creating her myth. Marlene is not Marlene. Marlene is me. She knows that very well, and every year she sends me her most recent photo with the same words: ''I was nothing without you. I am nothing without you.'' '
Joseph Von Sternberg

'He was my absolute lord . . . He possessed me from head to foot, and he knew it . . . My master! He kept me on a lead, like a dog. He was the one who undid the lead, not me!'
Marlene Dietrich

'If she'd had nothing but her voice, she would still have had something to break your heart with . . . Doesn't matter! She can put it together again for you! . . . She knows more about love than anybody.'
Ernest Hemingway

'There aren't ten commandments on love. Just one — love unconditionally!'
Marlene Dietrich

'I love you all the time. I forget you sometimes just as I forget that my heart is beating. But it doesn't stop beating . . . The only difference is that you are beautiful and I am ugly.'
Ernest Hemingway

'Beauty comes from within. That sounds horrible, but it's true.'
Marlene Dietrich

'Orson Welles accepted my adoration and devotion calmly . . . When I saw him and spoke to him, I felt like a plant that had just been watered.'

'Garbo, Hayworth, Monroe . . . They were all pleasant, ordinary girls until their Pygmalions came along and swallowed them whole . . . These Minotaurs then regurgitated creatures who, they claim, were the incarnations of their ideals and their imaginations, but who often completely contradicted their basic nature.'

'What is important is to build a cocoon around one's heart.'

MARLENE DIETRICH

'Just before filming the series "The Streets of San Francisco", Karl Malden was asked what he thought of his new partner. His reply was: "It's Kirk's son! That's good enough." '

'My father came to see me in a Shakespeare play while I was at college. As we were leaving, he said to me, "Son! I feel a lot easier about your future now. You're so bad it's perfectly obvious you'll never make it as an actor." '

'After I'd been playing my character in "The Streets of San Francisco" for a while, I went to parties in the evenings, and when they slowly threatened to turn into orgies, people would look at me in horror and scream "a cop". This happened to me on more than one occasion.'

'Men these days are all emasculated, and women are partly to blame . . . We live in a repressive age. No sex, no alcohol, no tobacco, no calories. First we lack something, then we explode — and it's always our partners who try it out first.'

'It's one hell of a job fighting off all those rumours. And it's no way for a couple to live their lives. As soon as you hear the slightest bit of tittle-tattle, you should immediately go and reassure your partner.'

'I don't own a revolver or a rifle. I've been arguing for arms control for years.'

'The American press thought my film "Falling Down" was ambiguous, and in a way encouraged people to take justice into their own hands. (A similar kind of controversy surrounded "Fatal Attraction" and "Basic Instinct".) The character I played is ambiguous, and I like this ambiguity — because life is ambiguous.'

'As an artist, I have a responsibility to hold a mirror up to society. It's less reassuring like that, but I enjoy pushing things to the limit to see how far the public is prepared to accept me.'

'I like films which involve a high degree of risk and venture into new territory. I don't believe that the cinema always has to reflect morally and socially correct values. A sense of realism is also important.

'Bad guys are simply more entertaining. Everyone has a little devil inside them. Sure, society wants to encourage us to behave in a civilised manner, but there is a part in everybody which would sometimes just like to do something really crazy.

'I took the lead role in "Hunt for the Green Diamond" as the Jack Cotton figure is closer to my own character than any of my other roles. He is a slightly twisted guy with a good sense of humour.'

'When I began to play young male leads, my father used to say to me, "I hope the public will one day find out about the treacherous character you hide behind your angel face." I think his wish has come true!'

'I want to carry on doing quality things.'

MICHAEL DOUGLAS

'I think Steve McQueen and Robert Redford have a good chance to become the "John Wayne" of the future. And certainly that great guy whose name has escaped me, but you know who I mean. "Do you mean Clint Eastwood?" That's the one. He will take my place.'   *John Wayne*

'The character he plays in the Westerns we have done together is modelled on what Clint is like in real life — slow and calm, like a cat. On the set, he does what he has to do, then he goes to sleep in a corner.'   *Sergio Leone*

'He looks as if he is made of steel, but in fact he wouldn't hurt a fly. "In the middle of winter once," says Jane Brolin, who has known him for 35 years, "he dived into the freezing water of a swimming pool to save a scarab!" There is no housekeeper at his home — he does everything himself. As far as the cooking and the washing up go, he's in a class of his own. I've seen him wash the same glass three times!'

'He doesn't realise he's a star. He lives in a town where the most minor starlets feels demeaned if she doesn't have a chauffeur-driven car for doing the shopping, but Clint drives his old van to work. He doesn't have any bodyguards or servants either.'   *A collaborator*

'It's true I play less talkative characters, but that's because economy is more eloquent than gesticulations; it also holds true if you're trying to express subtle ideas. In a good film, the audience think along with the story; in a second-rate film, the audience have to have everything explained.'

'Analysis is the actor's enemy. Don Siegel taught me to trust my instincts and to move fast. Sergio Leone taught me how to walk, to talk, to stay silent, to glare at someone with positive loathing, and to smoke dreadful cigarillos — and I'm not even a smoker . . .!'

'Specialists never stop going on about the death of the Western, when what really matters is not the *genre* but the storyline. In "Unforgiven", I demonstrate the consequences of violence, unlike other films which glorify or vulgarise it. If I thought my films encouraged people to be violent, I would not make them. I loathe drugs and pornography, and I am not in the least way violent. I even agree with banning firearms!'

'The success I have had in a particular type of role might encourage me to carry on in that direction. But I need to find out what I am capable of in other fields. (When you want to go for a swim in a swimming pool but don't know if you can swim or not, the only way of finding out is to jump in.) I don't like comfort; it stops you developing. I don't want people to write on my gravestone "He made twenty crime films and fifteen Westerns . . ." I've also sung songs and made records! Placido Domingo can sleep peacefully at night though! If I ever lay my hands on them, I'll dump them straight into the ocean!'

CLINT EASTWOOD

'If you want to be an actor, you go to Hollywood or New York. I tossed a coin. It came down New York. Then I tossed again. If you're going to be poor, it's better to be in the sun than the snow.'

The short bald man in the office looks at me as if he has just found a snake in his soup. He says to me, 'You're not the type we're interested in. But what would you say to a contract? Say, $150 a week?' I replied at once that I couldn't possibly afford that much.

'I started off with small roles on TV. At the same time, I learned carpentry out of books, and ten years later I still do it. As I was working for rich people, I was never unemployed. That way, I could take the jobs I liked. I didn't need to make a film just to eat.'

'Being an actor is the easiest way of prolonging childhood.'

'Indiana Jones is great fun to act as it is the total dream of the little guy.'

'It's OK playing him in two or three films, but no more. After that, you should call Roger Moore.'

'My job is being an assistant. I assist someone who wants to tell a story. Like the assistant petrol pump attendant assists the leading petrol pump attendant. Except that I've got millions of customers to see to.'

'The cinema is a powerful medium. We've got to be careful about what we make it say . . . Americans have paid dearly for the dreams which the cinema has aroused in them. After having heroism forced down their throats, they thought that they too were heroes. That's how they ended up in Vietnam.'

'Two's a couple, three's a group, four's a crowd.'

'I like small parties, not the never-ending Hollywood evenings. If I don't go to heaven when I die, I have this fear that purgatory will be like a discotheque!'

'I don't see how people find me attractive. I can't even bear to look at myself in the mirror in the morning.'

'The scar on my chin? I'd set off one morning in my old Volvo, and while I was trying to put my safety belt on, I ran into a lamppost. The car was a write-off. I got this scar on my chin, but I was within a whisker of being killed.'

'But it may be more interesting to go looking for mystery than to describe me as the relatively ordinary guy that I am.'

HARRISON FORD

'He was a gentleman, a true gentleman . . . He always got to his feet and brought me over a chair. I know I got on his nerves, because he used to spend days waiting for me to turn up — but he used to say that, once she was there, she caught up on lost time a thousand times!'
'I saw something of my father in him and, as Freud would say, there's nothing wrong with that! Far from it!'

Marilyn Monroe

'Clark loves playing practical jokes over the telephone! Pretend you don't recognise him! It makes him so happy!' was Carole Lombard's advice. Their decisive meeting had already taken place at a 'gag party' where Carole had lain down on a stretcher laughing. 'If I was a doctor, I would prescribe Gable with all meals!' said Clark. 'If I was Gable,' she replied, 'I'd try and remain in one piece!'

He had to save Myrna Loy from a blazing plane in the course of a film he was making. The fire got out of control. 'Cut!' shouted the director to let the firefighters pull Myrna from the flames. 'Keep rolling!' said Clark. 'I'll get her!' And he did!

This great seducer, a peasant's son, nonetheless had two handicaps: teeth that had been ruined by eating poor quality food and huge protruding ears. 'Like garage doors!' he used to quip.

'You'd think that if he flapped his ears he'd have taken off,' whispered a cameraman. 'We used to tape them back or blacken them up so they didn't pick up so much light; they also paid for him to have a completely new set of teeth.'

'His false teeth bothered me so much that I could hardly keep a straight face during our kissing scenes.'

Vivien Leigh

'When I had to act in my first love scene, I was frightened to death. The Director wanted me to have that longing expression on my face, so I thought of a huge rare steak. It worked so well that I've used the same trick ever since.'

'Everyone saw me in the role of Rhett Butler except me. I was one of the last to read "Gone with the Wind" — that is, until Spencer Tracy called across, "Hi, Rhett!". The role was far too big a mouthful for me — I didn't even fancy a tiny crumb. I went off to persuade the author to say that I was the worst choice imaginable . . . Then I found out I'd got the part from the newspapers!'

'Clark Gable was elected 'King of the Cinema' by millions of voters in the major newspapers. He was the Number 1 star in the Number 1 studio in Hollywood! Metro Goldwyn-Meyer who controlled 90% of the stars!'

'Me, direct?' he said after a career lasting thirty years. 'I don't now how to act yet!'

'I will know I've reached the top the day I can bring myself to throw my false teeth through Louis B Mayers' window (boss of MGM).'

CLARK GABLE

'I saw how clumsy he was and I looked at his large, hook nose, and wondered how this poor young man could possibly imagine he had any kind of future in acting.' *Arthur Miller 1965*

'He concentrates so hard that he transmits a sort of electric current to whoever he is acting with.' *Robert Redford*

'I had no trouble playing a virgin in "The Graduate" at the age of 31 as I still felt traumatised by my acne, my protruding nose on my over-long face — and above all my shortness, on which I blamed all my failures . . . I would have taken Robert Redford and Warren Beatty parts if I'd had their looks.'

'There came a moment when I accepted I was a masculine Barbra Streisand.'

'As far as Robert Redford is concerned, I have discovered through working with him how much nicer I am than him.'

'I belong to a family of halfwits with peculiar-looking heads, who became actors by mistake.'

'I've always been on the outside: I wasn't good-looking . . . girls didn't go for me. I decided to be an actor. The worst thing to do is to try to fight your own destiny.'

'I hope I don't bring back an Oscar tomorrow. (Hoffman had been nominated for "The Graduate".) It would really depress me to win as I don't deserve it.'

'An actor must defend his character just as a lawyer defends his client, even if he knows he's guilty.'

To try out the character in "Tootsie", Dustin went out into the streets dressed as a woman. 'It was then that I realised how often men looked past me over my shoulder looking for a woman who was prettier than me.'

'The best working relations I ever had were in "Kramer vs Kramer". We did come to blows while we were filming, it is true, but that's inevitable. That's how you bring the best out of people.'

DUSTIN HOFFMAN

'It wasn't just his remarkable electric-blue eyes and close-cropped, ash-grey hair over a perfectly-formed cranium. He had something of the tiger about him. There was also something about his powerful, athletic physique that suggested a wild animal ready to leap up or attack at any moment.'

'I think what summed Steve up was the fact that you felt he was dangerous. With the exception of Marlon Brando, I can hardly think of a cinema actor with more innate magnetism than Steve. You never knew what he was going to say or do next. That was what made him so exciting on screen.'

Ali McGraw

'Steve McQueen's performance in ''Papillon'' was extraordinary. Perhaps it was the best performance of his career. He was much better than me in that film. He was so deeply involved in it that I felt my own contribution was artificial.'

Dustin Hoffman

'He stayed loyal through thick and thin. He was the one I called when I no longer wanted to speak to anyone, and also the one who came to see me when he had already escaped from the world. The two of us could spend hours together without feeling the need to speak — the comfort of one another's presence was enough to calm our anxieties and sorrows.' *Paul Newman*

'He gives the impression that acting is easy — and that means real talent.' *Richard Attenborough*

'While we were making ''The Great Escape'', my motorbike was so fast that they couldn't find anyone to play the German motor cyclist who had to chase after me. Eventually, the director made me put on the soldier's uniform and I chased myself!'

'My wife, Neile, claims that I would have been impossible to live with if I'd brought home an Oscar! She's delighted that I lost.'

'The world can continue to go round and survive, and it can certainly do without my suggestions and those of other actors.'

'I would much prefer to spend an evening with the racing driver Stirling Moss than a whole night with Marilyn Monroe.'

STEVE MCQUEEN

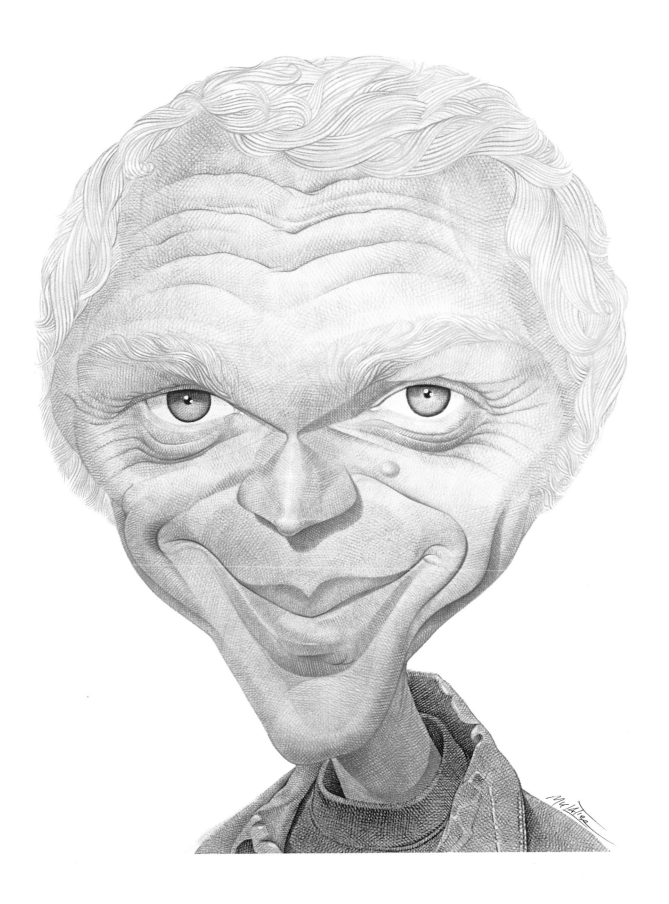

'To work with her was a fantastic experience. It was like being on an escalator: you caught up with her, she would move higher up, you kept up with her, and finally both got to the top.

Montgomery Cliff

'Deep below the surface of her skin, she has a layer of soft, damp flesh that other women do not have. In the dark, you can see her skin glowing.'

Her masseur

'It's almost as if she had no back. Her curves went in all directions, her flesh undulated . . .'

Jane Russell

'The dresses she wore had such plunging necklines that it looked as if she had jumped straight into them, and got her feet caught in the shoulder straps.'

One of her partners

The surgeon performing the appendicitis operation found a short message on Marilyn's tummy: 'Only remove what you have to. And please! Just a tiny little scar!'

'Why do men get so excited by a girl in a sweater? If you take the sweater off, what's left?'

'A woman can love with a new love each man she falls in love with — as long as there aren't too many of them.'

'Sex is part of Nature and I get on fine with Nature.'

'When journalists asked me why I posed nude, and I replied, "I was hungry", they thought that was smart. But at least I was able to pay the rent and buy myself some food. When they asked me, "What do you put on when you go to bed?" and I replied "Chanel No 5", they thought that was smart, too, although I was trying to give a tactful reply to a vulgar question. I tell the truth, but no one believes me.'

'Don't you mind posing in the nude?' 'No. Why? The studio was boiling.'

'Did you put anything on before you posed?' 'Yes. The radio.'

'What decided you to take acting lessons?' 'Seeing myself on screen.'

She was exactly three days late for a photo session, and ten minutes early. 'It's not me that's late. It's the others that are in such a rush! I was mentally with you at nine o'clock. I can't go as fast as them. They jump into their cars and rush home. There's no let up . . . Perfection takes time.'

'Nobody ever told me I was pretty when I was little. You should always tell little girls they're pretty, even when they aren't!'

MARILYN MONROE

'We shall certainly continue to make James Bond films until he dies, and possibly after that.'
Albert R Broccoli, producer and one-time manufacturer of graves

'Roger Moore's performances as Bond are as diametrically opposed to mine as can be. He opts immediately for humour and parody. That's his choice. Roger is a friend of mine and, certainly as far as Bond is concerned, I have no proprietorial instincts.'
'Roger and I have yet to play in the same film. It could be something like Doctor Jekyll and Mr Hyde. To take account of our susceptibilities, they'd have to put a name like Roger Seanmooreconnery at the top of the posters. That might be a bit long, though . . .' *Sean Connery*

'At MGM the make-up artist always had problems with me. When I was very young they tried to make my youthful, smooth looks more interesting. Today they try to make my interesting looks smoother and more youthful.'

'After doing the ''Saint'' for six or seven years, the idea of getting caught up in a TV series did not exactly fill me with enthusiasm. However, the producer of ''The Persuaders'' was very persuasive, saying that even the Queen and England both needed the money . . . Tony Curtis and I were equally involved in the project. Tony saw us a bit like Laurel and Hardy, although he never said which of us was the fat one.'

'Yes, yes, of course I do the majority of stunts myself. The other day I even played a love scene myself.'

'When I was finally selected as Bond, I had to loose weight, diet, exercise and cut my hair very short. I think I lost more weight at the hairdresser than through diet and exercise.'

'Sean was tougher than me as Bond. When he announced ''I'm going to kill you'', you believed him straight away. I sounded more as if I was offering to buy someone a drink at the bar.'

'Problems? Well, it's always the same: collecting your paypacket from Cubby Broccoli on a Friday is the most difficult problem of all.'

ROGER MOORE

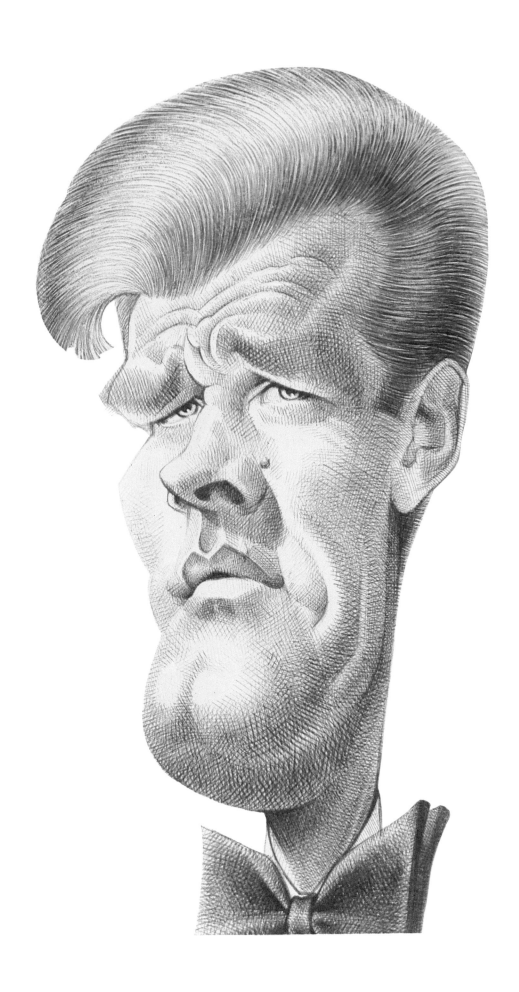

'He's the only person who can smile one of those foolish smiles and give you goose pimples.'
'Jack Nicholson is unquestionably the greatest actor in Hollywood today.'   *Stanley Kubrik*

'He's a wonderful person, and I admire him enormously. He is so keen not to be labelled a star that he takes small parts as well as big ones.'   *Robert Redford*

'That's very shrewd of you,' his friend Tony Curtis admitted to him once. 'That way, when you are eventually obliged to take small roles, no one will notice the difference.'

'Jack Nicholson's eyebrows alone deserve an Oscar nomination.'   *Philadelphia Daily News*

'He has achieved a staggering technical mastery as an actor. If there was such a thing as an ideal world, Jack would be the ideal actor.''   *George Miller, Director of ''The Witches of Eastwick''*

'I was poor, really poor . . . If you've learned to combat hunger, thirst and the misery of wearing threadbare shirts and shoes with holes in them, it's a good training later on for fighting against a script that's going wrong, poor dialogue or an untalented director.'

'It was the first public screening of ''Easy Rider'' at Cannes in 1969. I was sitting in the auditorium, and I suddenly felt a shiver and my hair stood on end. It was a delicious and terrible experience all at the same time. I was overwhelmed with pleasure — and at the same time with disappointment — and I said to myself, ''Well, here we are then! I'm a film star!'' '

'An Oscar is like spaghetti sauce: if you get it, fine; if you don't, just be patient.'

'Me, the biggest American star? No way! There are other big stars — Dustin, Warren, Clint . . . You must mean ''the *greatest* actor''!'

'The thing I miss most from the past? What I used to weigh!'

JACK NICHOLSON

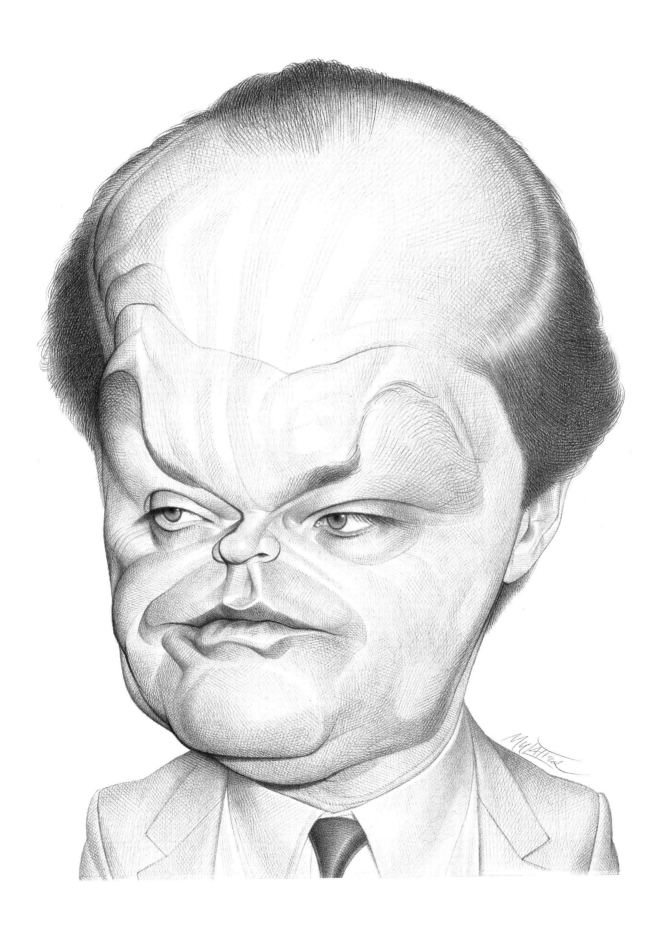

'These days, Robert Redford is the one and only.'   *Marlene Dietrich*

'When I went to school, I used to pass in front of the Fox studios. One day, I saw a huge piece of sky scenery hanging in mid-air with painted clouds. I said to myself, "They must be crazy! They paint the sky, and all the time they've got a real one overhead!" '

'I was born a very ordinary guy with yellowy hair. And as I'm a slightly sombre individual deep down, I feel I am brown. Even black sometimes. Nobody ever said I was good-looking when I was young and unemployed.'

'When I look at myself, it always makes me feel uneasy. I have this idea that if we worry too much about ourselves, we get lost. It isn't enough to be able to act; you've got to be able to win as well. My looks have prevented the full expression of my talent. The predominant image is glamour — the cosmetic bit. Whatever work I'm doing, people don't see the character I'm playing; they simply see the handsome Redford playing a character. When an actor involves himself in serious issues, he becomes no longer credible, and he is even less so if he is not good-looking. People only see the beautiful object.'

'Vast expanses of this country which have remained untouched are now condemned. It's in our nature — our society has moved firmly in the direction of development and profit. And despite the fear of toxic substances and the problems of pollution, we carry on building. But we shall lose many of our traditions and cultural roots that way. Do we want to preserve our culture or abandon it to the profit motive? Most people who feel symapthetic towards the fate of aboriginal inhabitants are the first to sell their houses to property developers.'

'People want industrial comfort. They refuse to sacrifice comfort for the sake of nature. Human life as we know it will disappear. Good to know that I won't be around then.'

'Unlike Robert de Niro who sleeps with his roles, I leave mine in the dressing room back at the theatre.'

'I am not interested in political responsibility. Certainly not for the time being. It is considered acceptable to hunt down public figures on the assumption that there must be something unresolved about them. Our private lives are seriously affected by it. Moreover, the public do not want to hear themselves saying disturbing things. We make a choice, then, and put up with flatterers by feeding the illusion that we are in a perfect, strong, brave, bold country. I refuse to be part of this idiocy.'

ROBERT REDFORD

'Arnold is moving increasingly in the direction of a Cary Grant-style career.'
John McTiernan, Director of "Last Action Hero"

'Question: Who is the biggest film star? — Schwarzenegger or Sir Laurence Olivier? There's only one answer to this: Arnold. The key word in the question is "star".
Next question: Who is the better actor? Schwarzenegger or Olivier? Since we are comparing one of the most popular stars of the eighties with the actor of the century, the decision should fall on Olivier. But don't be so sure — it's true, I wouldn't want to see Schwarzenegger play Hamlet. But at the same time I wouldn't want to see Olivier as the Terminator . . .
William Goldman

'Money doesn't make me happy. I really couldn't care less whether I have 48 or 50 Million Dollars.'

'I've rarely known a director to complain about good box office receipts. They're more important than anything else. I'm not interested in being in a film that is only going to be seen by four people.'

'I want the public to distinguish between the characters I play on screen and the person I really am. I am not Conan and I am not the Terminator, and I don't walk down the street holding a gun because I'm out to settle scores with people whose faces I don't remember.'

'I enjoy life enormously. I'm the sort of person that puts firecrackers in people's cigars.'

'You must join my new club,' Stallone said to me. 'What club?' I said. 'A club just for men,' he replied. 'Like the old days. Just men. We can sit back and smoke cigars and pipes, and have a good time.' 'It's the worst thing you can do,' I told him. 'We live at a very sensitive age with women fighting for equality. I don't go along with half the ideas they come up with, but that kind of club would offend every intelligent woman in the country. I will never come! If you only want to see people like that, invite them round to your home. That's what I do!'

'I love to get orders from women. I used to be the barbaric one, but since I married Maria, I even clean the windows, unfortunately I never get them as clean as she does. When I go over them again to do Maria a favour, I'm usually too vigorous. The glazier gives me a discount — he's a fan.'

'When life begins to run out, in about ten years' time, I shall re-assess my life and decide what image I want to leave behind me — political, cultural, philanthropic, I don't now yet. If I passed away tomorrow, my gravestone would have a line saying "He enjoyed himself." '

ARNOLD SCHWARZENEGGER

'I was four when I first went to see a psychiatrist. After a chat he said: the kid is fine, perhaps there's something wrong with the parents.'

'I grew up in a part of New York where kids only have two options: either to end up in the electric chair or in show business. Looks like I've been pretty lucky so far.'

'At high school my teachers thought that out of all the pupils I was the only one most likely to end up in the electric chair.'

'Comedies work if the star's sense of humour is made use of. Otherwise, the actor looks a complete fool.'

'My fans don't want to see me make a fool of myself. They want to see me doing things, being hurt and hitting people. They do *not* want to see me fooling around. For that sort of thing, they've got Schwarzenegger who can move from one style to the next without causing a revolution of any sort.'

'I never think about my role. Should I ever find myself approaching a role in an intellectual manner, I know that I'm in the wrong film.'

'People think my intelligence has its limits. I just don't look intelligent.'

Perhaps I look stupid and sometimes I do crazy things. But I have hired two guards who will lock me up and send me straight to prison if I start thinking about marriage.'

'I go out with lots of women because I have a dreadful tendency to get attached very quickly. I also change partners as often as possible.'

'Because I'm strong, people think I haven't got a brain. It's the same for women with beautiful breasts. But despite my muscles, I've written three books and twenty-five scripts.'

'I want to be fancied for my brain not my brawn.'

'I think people look at me as a cave man who rolls around in the mud and walks around chewing on a piece of meat. I suppose people don't understand that my life is more mental than physical. I am where I am because my mental concept has been fulfilled. There are people who have more muscles than I will ever have.

'I shouldn't complain if I had to make Rocky-films until the end of my life. But come to Rocky 30, I would have problems getting into the ring in a wheelchair.'

SYLVESTER STALLONE

'Bastard! Weakling!' John Ford used to shout at him on the set of the first film they did together. 'It was for his own good,' the director was to say later of the man who had once been a property master and who became his favourite actor and friend. 'I had to push John Wayne as far as he could go to get the best out of him. Either he was going to crack or he was going to make a name for himself. He didn't crack!'

In 1970, he finally won the only Oscar of his career for his role as the one-eyed sheriff in ''True Grit''. 'If I'd known, I'd have put a patch over my eye 35 years ago.'

Left-wing students at Harvard did not hesitate to award him the prize for the worst actor of the year. They challenged him to come and free Maureen O'Hara who they claimed to be holding prisoner. Wayne arrived at the University in a tank with an escort of marines and a military fanfare, and was greeted with applause by the good-natured students.'

The director of Wayne's latest film, ''The Shootist'', asked the great man to take his trousers off, as indicated in the script. 'There's not going to be a naked bottom in any film I'm in,' he replied, 'especially if it's mine.'

' ''The Wild Bunch'' is a film in very poor taste. It would have been good, though, if there hadn't been so much blood.'

'I received three pieces of advice from my father. First, always keep your word; second, a gentleman never insults anybody intentionally; third, don't go around looking for trouble, but if you get into a fight, make sure you win it.'

'I'll stay in the saddle until I fall off.'

'My only enemy is Big C, but as usual I'll get my own way.'

JOHN WAYNE

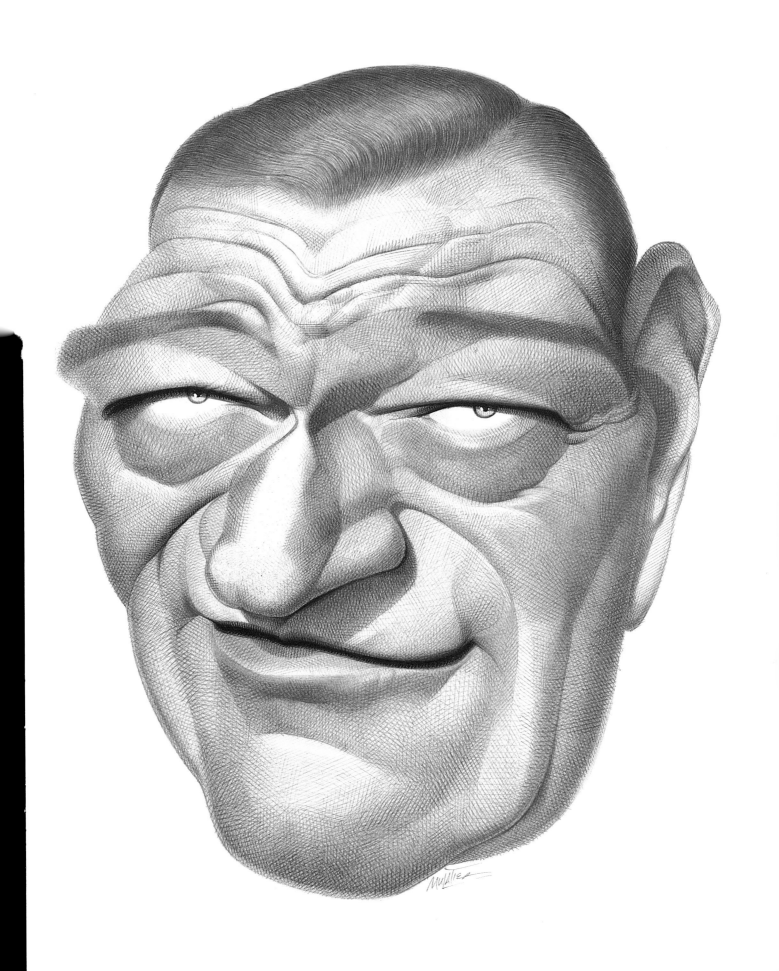

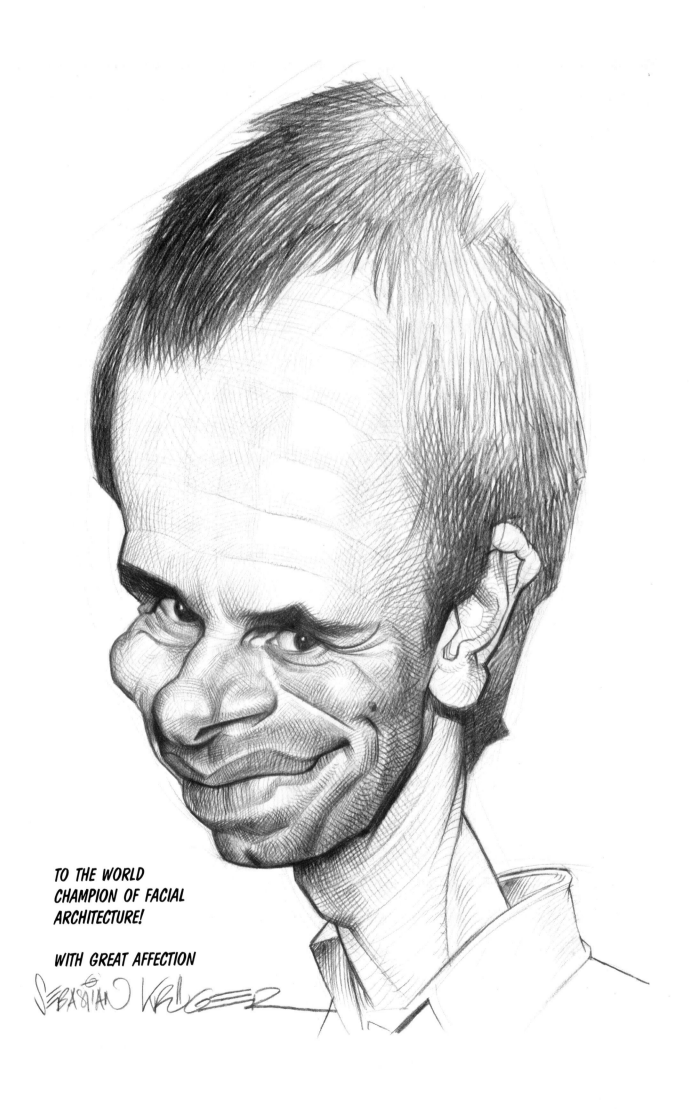

TO THE WORLD
CHAMPION OF FACIAL
ARCHITECTURE!

WITH GREAT AFFECTION

© 1993 by Ehapa Verlag GmbH, Stuttgart, Germany — Jean Mulatier

This edition first published by Ravette Books Limited 1993

Printed and bound for Ravette Books Limited
8 Clifford Street
London W1X 1RB
An Egmont Company
by Cantz'sche Druckerei, Ostfildern/Germany

ISBN 1 85304 363 X